I0468237

HOW TO TRADE THE HL30 TECHNIQUE- FOREX DAY TRADING

HOW TO DAY TRADE YOUR FAVORITE CURRENCY PAIR AND MAKE 20 TO 60 PIPS ALMOST EVERY DAY

By

JOSEPH FIBONACCI

Copyright © 2014

www.howtomakemoneytradingforex.com

INTRODUCTION

Before we begin, and I'm sure you're already aware of this... I highly recommend testing out this trading strategy and any other strategy that you are not familiar with on a demo account or paper trade it. Do not use real money when testing out these trading strategies.

And if you have been trading for some time, you already know that there is no holy Grail. It's not possible that one trading strategy will work in every single market condition every time the markets move up or down. Each technique is specific to certain conditions and certain types of market environments that are optimum for the technique itself.

The strategy you are going to learn in this report specifically works in certain market environments outlined below. Using this technique on another timeframe or in a different type of market condition will obviously generate different results than I claim. It is very important that you use the technique exactly as I lay it out here in this report. Otherwise you're going to get different results than I claim.

This technique is just as susceptible to potential failed trades as any other strategy out there. The way to improve this technique just like any other is to understand it so well, that you know it like the back of your hand. Once you understand the technique, the optimum trading environments to execute this technique and when to avoid using it, you will certainly improve the results you gain from using this technique.

Using the HL30, it is very possible that you can earn 20, 40, 60 and even up to 120 pips in the first few hours of a new trading day. Obviously every day is different and I cannot guarantee that this will happen every single day. And again it is vital that you understand the technique so well that you know when to use it and when not to use it which will also improve your chances of having more successful trading days than losing days.

*I have included a bonus video trading course absolutely FREE. This video course compliments all of the trading strategies you will learn in this book. It's simply easier to learn the strategies by watching a video. This is available to you right now. Please visit the web link below to get started now

http://the4xcoach.com/amzminicourse/

TABLE OF CONTENTS

(This is set up to only show Heading 1 so the main chapter headings but not sub headings.)

LEGAL NOTES

The information provided in this report is for educational purposes only. It is not a recommendation to buy or sell nor should it be considered investment advice. You are responsible for your own trading decisions. Past performance is not indicative of future results, as returns may vary according to market conditions.

Trading in foreign exchange is speculative and may involve the loss of principal; therefore, assets placed in any type of forex account should be risk capital funds that if lost will not significantly affect one's personal financial well being.

This is not a solicitation to invest, and you should carefully consider the suitability of your financial situation prior to making any investment or entering into any transaction.

Trading foreign exchange on margin carries a high level of risk, and may not be suitable for all investors. The high degree of leverage can work against you as well as for you.

Before deciding to invest in foreign exchange you should carefully consider your investment objective, level of experience and risk appetite.

The possibility exists that you could sustain a loss of some or all of your initial investment and therefore you should not invest money that you cannot afford to lose.

You should be aware of all the risks associated with foreign exchange trading and seek advice from an independent financial adviser if you have any doubts.

By Federal Mandate, Foreign Currency Traders Must Read This First:

Before deciding to trade real money in the Retail Forex market, you should carefully consider whether this is the right choice for you.

Things to consider are your investment objectives, level of experience and risk appetite. Most importantly, do not invest money you cannot afford to lose, i.e., don't trade forex with money you need to survive.

Limitation of Liability:

You understand and agree that under no circumstances will Joseph Fibonacci, the4xcoach.com,
it's owners, staff, or members be held liable for any direct, indirect, consequential, incidental,

special or exemplary damages for any use of this information in this book or any linked contents, even if we are advised of the possibility of such damages.

Your only remedy is to discontinue use of this material. You waive the rights of lawsuit for any damage happened with this information. Information on any/all subjects and matters in this book is subject to change at any time. Joseph Fibonacci does not guarantee the accuracy of the information provided by it's owner's, staff, or members.

- Joseph Fibonacci.

Chapter 1. What you can expect from this book

Before we begin, and I'm sure you're already aware of this...

I highly recommend testing out this trading strategy and any other strategy that you are not familiar with on a demo account or paper trade it. Do not use real money when testing out these trading strategies.

And if you have been trading for some time, you already know that there is no holy Grail. It's not possible that one trading strategy will work in every single market condition every time the markets move up or down. Each technique is specific to certain conditions and certain types of market environments that are optimum for the technique itself.

The strategy you are going to learn in this report specifically works in certain market environments outlined below. Using this technique on another timeframe or in a different type of market condition will obviously generate different results than I claim. It is very important that you use the technique exactly as I lay it out here in this report. Otherwise you're going to get different results than I claim.

This technique is just as susceptible to potential failed trades as any other strategy out there. The way to improve this technique just like any other is to understand it so well, that you know it like the back of your hand. Once you understand the technique, the optimum trading environments to execute this technique and when to avoid using it, you will certainly improve the results you gain from using this technique.

Using the HL30, it is very possible that you can earn 20, 40, 60 and even up to 120 pips in the first few hours of a new trading day. Obviously every day is different and I cannot guarantee that this will happen every single day. And again it is vital that you understand the technique so well that you know when to use it and when not to use it which will also improve your chances of having more successful trading days than losing days.

The technique I am going to teach you is one that I use every day.

This particular technique is called the HL 30 technique. It is what me and my students call "the easiest Forex day trading technique ever" and once you learn how to use it, I'm sure you will agree that it is very easy to use and repeat every day for consistent profits.

This technique is purely technical. I'm not relying on any economic data however economic data does have an impact on the movement of price and will very often be the "fuel" for the move and my take profit levels. The HL30 trading system is designed to generate trade signals and to do so with the least amount of visual distraction. This basically means that the easier it is to identify and confirm a trade, the easier it is to quickly find and execute a trade order.

The set up is quite simple.

The challenge is to repeat it without any mistakes. If some of the components are missing or do not line up (confirmation), then there is no trade and I suggest waiting for the next opportunity. There are other times when all the criteria has been met and the trade could still fail. Often, this can happen inside of consolidation. But I have several methods that will help prevent failed trades.

You must exercise discipline when executing this trade. If the initial signal does not confirm, do not execute the trade!

Wait for the next one. I also recommend looking for this technique to set up a trade signal on at least four different currency pairs, perhaps the majors (EUR/USD, GBP/USD, USD/JPY, USD/CHF) because very often but not every single day, I can have two or three HL 30 trades that will result in up to 120 pips or more on a good day. Just the same there are days when I might not have any HL 30 signals and if you're going to build your trading business exclusively from using this technique, which many of my coaching students have, you have to accept that when there is no trade signal according to your system, you do nothing!

This is easier said than done but the mark of a true, skilled trader.

Now that we have that out of the way, let's move on...

(I have a video tutorial minicourse to show you how this technique works and how to improve the results by identifying the ideal conditions for this technique, understanding when to use it and when not to use it. To gain access to this minicourse please click the link below- it's totally free and complements this book)

http://the4xcoach.com/amzminicourse/

Chapter 2. The indicators: how to set up your charts

We begin with and always use this method on a 30 minute chart. When I developed this method, I noticed just like everyone else does, the quiet or slow period when a particular market is closed. For the majors, excluding the dollar yen, it is usually during the Asian session leading into the London session.

As I mentioned earlier, please use this technique exactly as I lay it out here for you. If you change any of the details, you will change the results. I know it's tempting to take a strategy and immediately start using other techniques or other components of other techniques and strategies, blending them all and mixing them up to the point where you have nothing that resembles what you started with. This is a very simple strategy and I recommend using it exactly as I describe.

The 30 minute chart has always produced the best results for me. I tested it out using a 15 minute chart and a one hour chart and this testing was done in a live market environment with my live account. I know that the 30 minute chart will produce the best results for you.

There are four basic candle patterns that will trigger a signal.

And were only going to use one indicator and that is the CCI indicator set at 14 on the 30 minute chart

The candle patterns that will signal an entry are Candle Patterns:

- Bullish or Bearish Engulfing

- Evening star

- Morning star

If you're new to candlestick patterns, I highly recommend that you stick to the picture-perfect candlestick patterns that are necessary for an HL 30 entry. I've often said that the picture-perfect candlestick patterns are the ones that will produce the best results and it's true.

Recently, one of my coaching students said that he actually felt guilty because it was so easy to make money using this technique as long as he waited for the picture-perfect candlestick patterns that triggered an HL 30 entry.

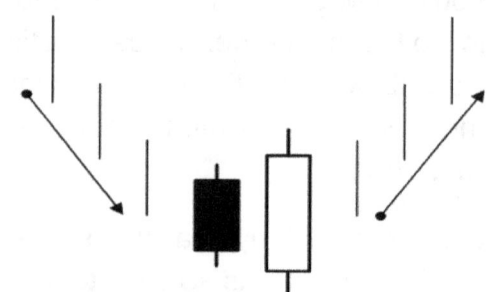

Bullish Engulfing Pattern

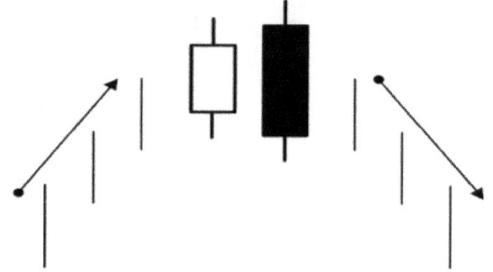

Bearish Engulfing Pattern

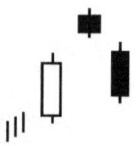

Evening Star Pattern

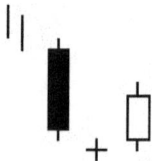

Morning Star Pattern

CHAPTER 3. THE STRUCTURE

What I'm actually doing when I execute this trade on a 30 minute chart is trading off of the previous day's high and low.

In order to determine where the start of a new day begins, I use the industry-standard which is the 5 PM Eastern time rollover period.

(NOTE: different brokers offer different pricing schedules/pip spreads. You may notice that your broker will widen the pip spread to a larger than normal amount making it not as profitable if you execute the trade within the first hour of a new trading day/ 5 PM to 6 PM Eastern time. If this is the case but you want to use this HL 30 technique exclusively for your trading strategy, I recommend contacting different brokers to find out what their pips spread is on the majors between these hours)

I will continue to repeat this because it's very important that you understand it, there are ways to improve this technique and to minimize the losses because you will experience losses but you can certainly minimize them by understanding the proper trading environment to execute this trade. As with anything else in life, experience is the only way to become successful.

Generally, if you were to only focus in on a 30 minute chart and never took a step back to see the overall larger picture such as the one hour, the four hour the daily charts to identify were key support and resistance levels are, you're going to do pretty well executing the HL 30. However occasionally price is going to run into key support and resistance levels on the larger time frames that you might not be able to see on a 30 minute chart. This is potentially a time when the HL 30 could fail. With each HL 30 that you execute, I highly recommend taking a look at the larger time frames to be aware of key support resistance levels or trending days.

Because were trading off of the previous days high or low, it's like trading in a short-term range of consolidation, and this trade is a reversal technique.

Please note, if consolidation continues, and I mean the same range of consolidation for more than one day, you might consider not trading HL 30 on the second or third day of the same consolidation.

The reason is that the longer consolidation continues in the same range, the less reliable some of the reversal signals become. Occasionally price will start spiking higher through resistance or lower through support but ultimately returning back inside of consolidation.

Those spikes could potentially stop you out on an HL 30.

I only recommend using the HL 30 at the beginning of a new consolidation range.

So you're probably asking how do you know if you're looking at the start of a new consolidation range?

Well the key point in the HL 30 is to trade off of the previous day's high and low but there is a specific condition that needs to be in place on that previous day.

There has to be some kind of trending move regardless of direction.

(For more detail please see some of the videos in the free minicourse as this will explain exactly what I'm talking about)

If there was no trending move on the previous day for the particular currency pair that you're going to trade, then that would most likely indicate that it's consolidation and as I mentioned earlier, if it's consolidation during the previous day that you're looking at, you do not want to execute the HL 30 again.

Ideal trading conditions

Okay, it's 5 PM New York time and you're looking at the EUR/USD and it's Tuesday, (or any other day during the week)

You notice that there was a slight trending day on Monday.

You will begin by identifying the high and the low of Monday's trading range.

Please keep in mind that every day is going to set up a different price structure. Some days price will close at the highs or the lows of the previous day and other days price will close in the middle of the previous day's trading range.

What you're specifically looking for is some kind of trending day on the previous day. It doesn't have to be a huge move as long as you can see a trending environment. Again that is condition or trading environment Rule Number One!

CHAPTER 4. THE SET UP

If the conditions and the trading environment are optimum to execute the HL 30, then we begin looking for the signal.

At the 5 PM rollover, mark off the previous day's high and low with a resistance and support line.

You then need to identify what I call "the 10 PIP range".

This 10 PIP range means that price needs to return to either support or resistance, let's take resistance for example.

If price is to qualify for the 10 PIP range then price needs to approach the previous day's high at least 10 pips below the previous day's high but it cannot exceed 10 pips above the previous day's high. (see image one and two)

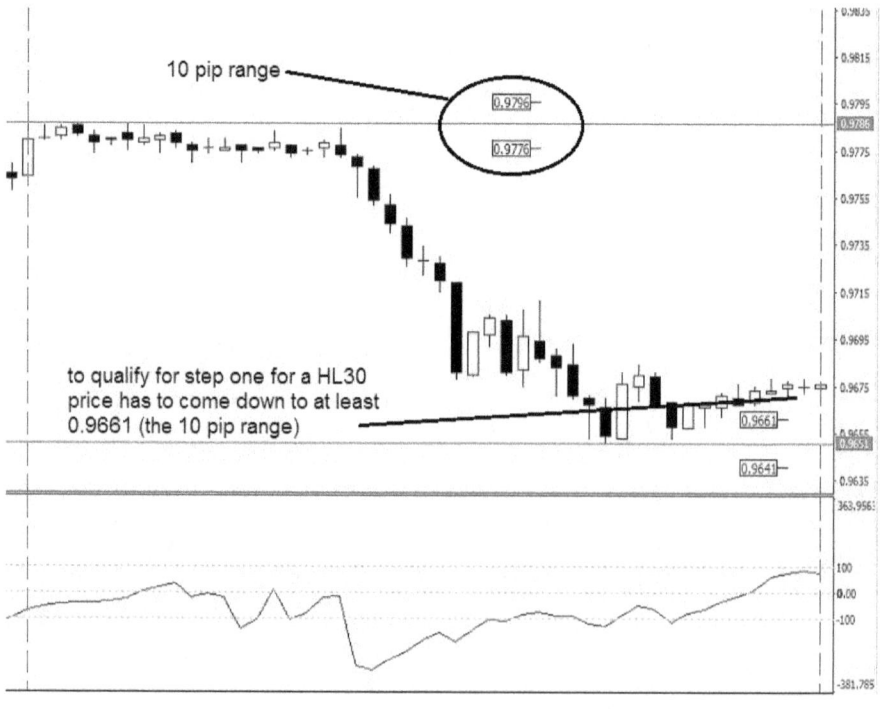

price has now moved down to the 10 pip range and the last candle is the reversal (the engulfing/ morning star pattern)

Now this technically is a 20 PIP range but I've always referred to as the 10 PIP range.

Just the same, if we were going to trade an HL 30 off of support then price needs to approach support within that 10 PIP range and this means that it needs to go down at least 10 pips above the previous day's support level but it cannot exceed 10 pips lower than the previous day's low.

If price does not approach the 10 PIP range in either direction, then we will not have an HL 30 to execute. It doesn't mean that it will not be a reversal, it's just that I will not executed with the parameters such as the take profit and stoploss for the HL 30.

In order to execute an HL 30 reversal trade, using the 20 pip stop in the 20 pip target, all of these conditions must be met and it all starts with the 10 PIP range.

Once we have price within the 10 PIP range, we then wait for a reversal signal candle. The reversal candle patterns or mentioned earlier.

Once we have a closed completed reversal candle pattern, we then confirm that signal with the CCI indicator. There cannot be any divergence. If there is it is not a qualified HL 30 trade!

For example, if we are trading a bounce off of support, a bullish HL 30, (see previous chart two) on the closed completed reversal candle pattern the CCI must print a higher reading than the previous day's low CCI reading. If it is lower, that would indicate divergence and we would have to pass on the trade. (Please see free minicourse videos to get a better understanding of divergence and the confirmation)

If everything confirms including the CCI, we get in on the close of that reversal signal candle.

The profit target is a 20 pip target (not including the spread) and the stoploss is 20 pips. These are the trade parameters for executing the HL 30 on the majors (EUR/USD, GBP/USD, USD/JPY, USD/CHF)

There is a way to maximize the results of each HL 30. I will discuss them later in in this report and I highly recommend watching the free minicourse videos which will walk you through the process of making up to 60 pips profits on each HL 30 when the conditions are perfect for these results.

But for now will just focus in on using the HL 30 with a 20 pip target 20 pip stop.

The 20 pip target with a 20 pip stop

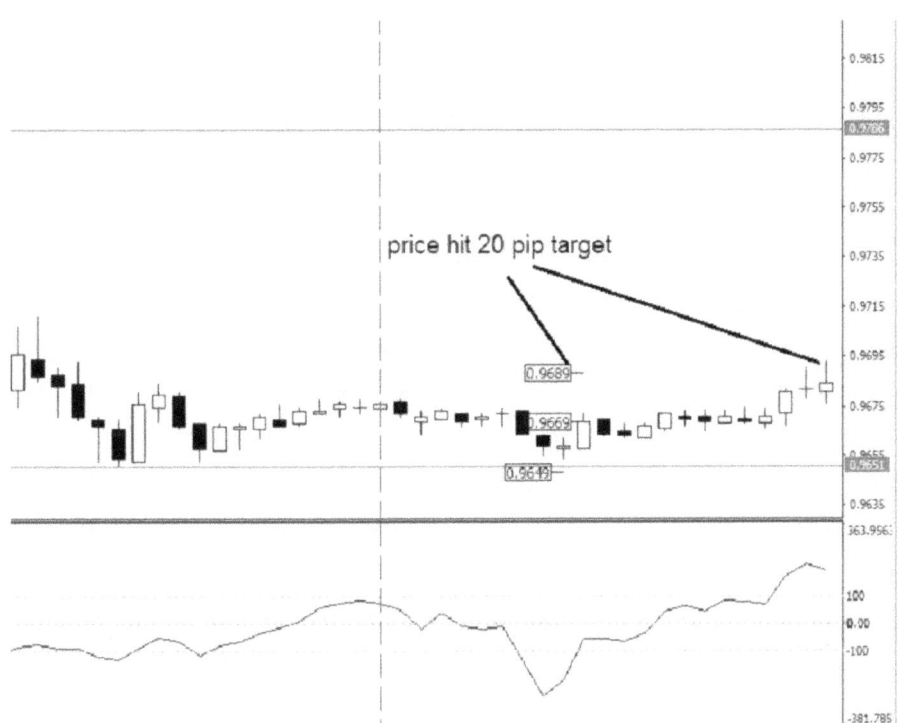

price hit 20 pip target

the 20 pip target hit

Confirming the trading environment

It's important to determine the current conditions. One way to avoid a possible failed trade is to look back not only at the previous day's high and low but you must also confirm that there was some kind of trending move on the previous day.

If the previous day was just more consolidation then I would avoid executing an HL30 altogether.

The next two charts show an example of a good trending day which is the right condition for a HL30 and the following chart shows a consolidation day which is not the right condition for a HL30

there IS a trend on this day so this would be the right condition for a HL30

a good trending environment

there is no trend on this day so this would not be
the right conditions for a HL30

not a good trending environment

CHAPTER 5. MORE EXAMPLES OF THE HL30 TRADE

Chart 1 EUR/USD 30 minute chart

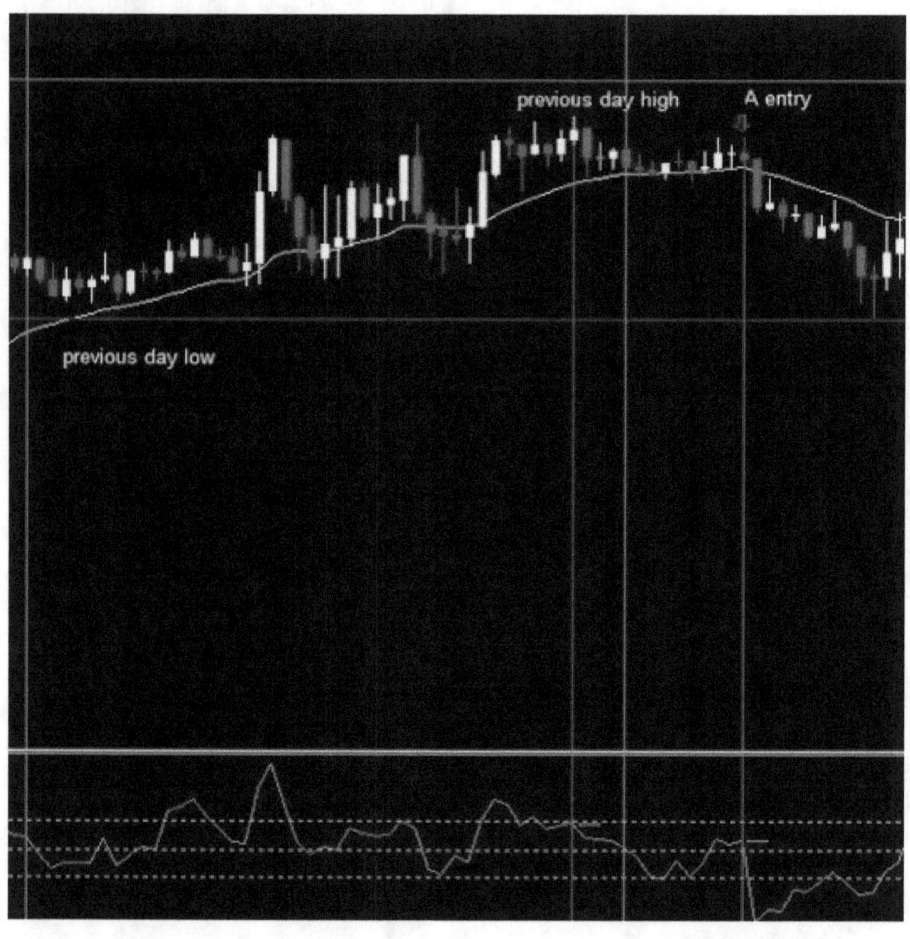

In this example we entered short on a bearish engulfing candle. In order for a signal to be confirmed, there must be a closed, completed candle pattern. (the entry was on the closed candle "A")

On the EUR/USD pair we are only looking to achieve 20 pips with the same size for a stop loss. If there happens to be a small rally in place then we will trail the trade for perhaps another 20 pips. If the price action has been somewhat muted and there is no economic data available then we would most likely look for a close target with in the nearest support or resistance range.

The set up requires that each day must be identified. We do this by adding a purple vertical line to each chart on the 30 minute time frame right at 5 pm New York time. This begins the new day. From this we can determine the high and the low of the previous day.

(the olive vertical lines are drawn in to highlight the CCI measurement on the signal candle compared to the high or low of the previous day)

In the EUR/USD example, price moved back up to the high of the previous day a few hours after the start of the new day.

Price must be within a 10 pip range to qualify as a test of support or resistance. This means that the candle that attempts to test the previous day high or low must be either within 10 pips short or beyond it. If it moves further, the trade is canceled.

The 10 pip rule is the same for all currencies when we use this strategy.

Once we have confirmed the price move or retest is within the 10 pip rule, we wait for the closed completed candle pattern.

In this case (previous EUR/USD chart 1) we confirmed that there was a bearish engulfing candle.

Before we enter, we need to check the CCI indicator.

As was the case on the EUR/USD chart 1 above, the closed completed bearish engulfing candle CCI reading printed a lower

CCI measurement than the CCI measurement when price made the new relative high from the previous day.

This is very important because if the CCI does not confirm then we have no trade.

In this case the confirmation was positive and we have a trade.

The entry is on the close of the candle pattern!

No delay or hesitation. The target on the EUR/USD is 20 pips and we use a 20 pip stop. If price continues to rally we will trail the trade to the next 20 pips if possible.

Chart 2 EUR/USD 30 minute

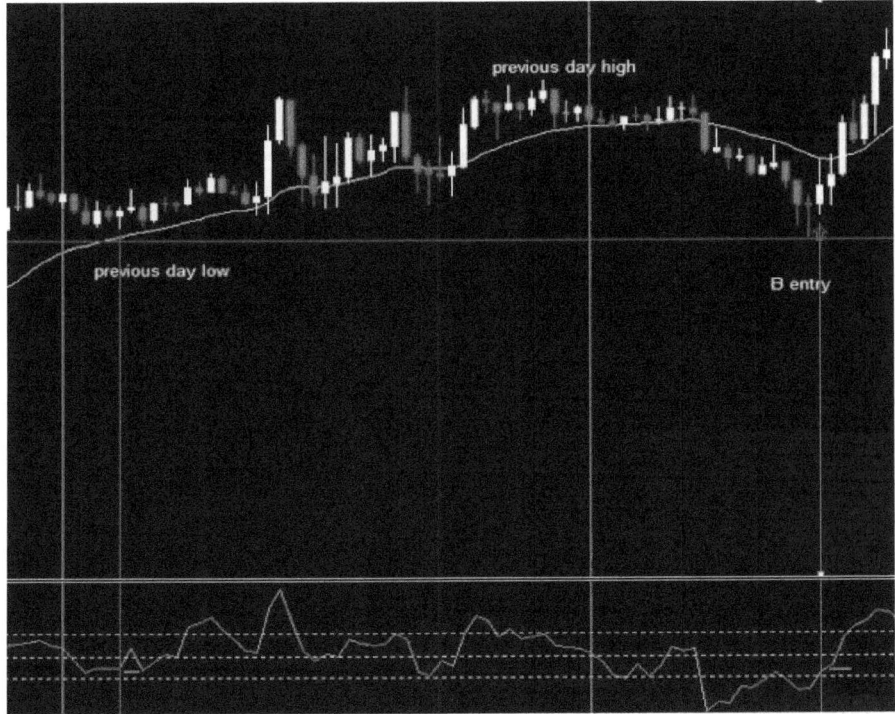

Now you might recognize this chart, it was the same pair on the same day.

After we shorted the EUR/USD and took profits, we waited to see how price would react when it returned to the previous days low (support).

As you can see it entered the 10 pips rule (zone) and then printed a bullish Morning star pattern with the CCI measuring a higher reading than the previous day low CCI measurement.

Again we took 20 pips and use the same size stop loss.

(please note that this opportunity does not happen all the time and this technique works best inside on consolidation)

Chart 3 GBP/USD 30 minute

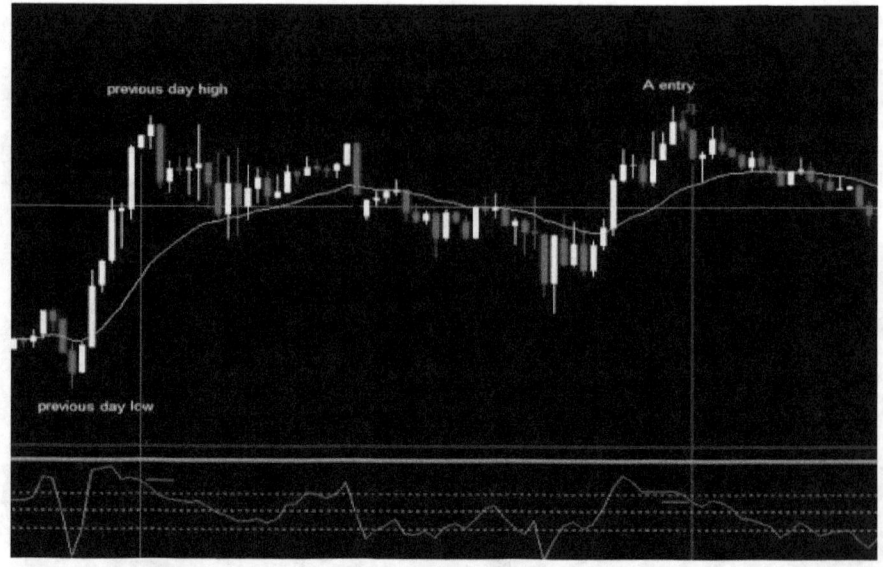

This trade is similar to the previous EUR/USD short trade.

We use the same candle patterns, wait for price to move to previous day high (within the 10 pip range) and look for the closed completed candle pattern. Once we see the completed candle pattern we confirm the CCI measurement and then place the trade immediately on the closed candle pattern. With the GBP/USD our profit targets are 20 pips and a 20 pip stop loss.

Chart 4 EUR/JPY 30 minute

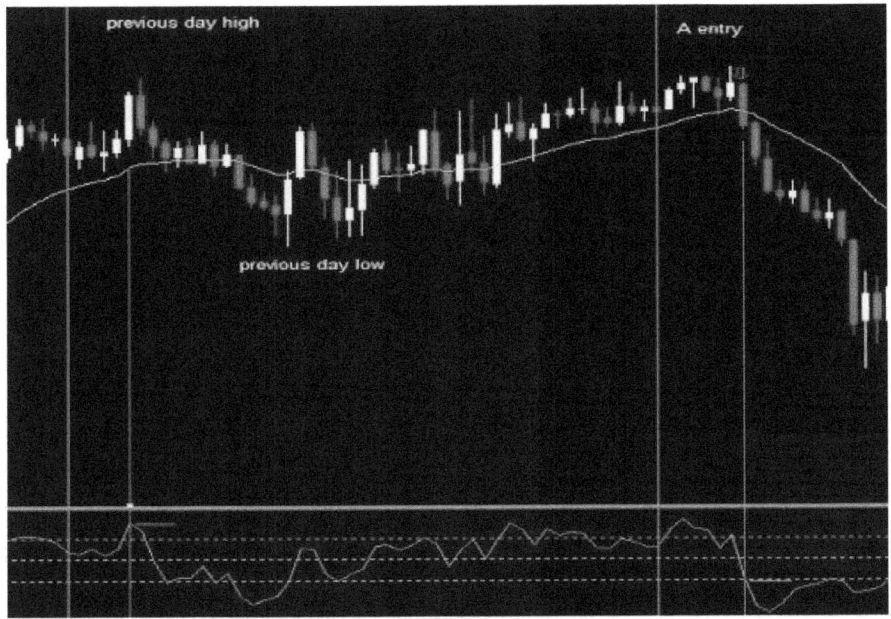

This trade was on the EUR/JPY. Again using the same criteria and confirmation.

The profit targets on this pair are 40 pip target and 40 pip stop loss (the yen crosses are larger targets and stops because they cover a greater distance

Chapter 6. Trading the HL30 around the News

There are a few key points I would like to share with you if you are considering using this strategy when economic data is set to be released.

If you find an HL 30 trading signal 30 minutes to one hour prior to major economic data I would suggest holding off on the trade and waiting until the data is released. It isn't so much because the trade will not work, it is that during economic data price can spike up or down more than the typical stop loss level we use on each HL 30 trade.

If you find that a signal has developed before major economic data and price has not hit its target at the time the data is released, it's possible to re-enter the trade once you have confirmation of the data and it supports the signal.

Please keep in mind that not all economic data is a trading opportunity. And very often an economic report can produce a very good trade one month but the next month not deliver anything at all but uncertainty.

Please remember regardless of whether or not the signal develops around the news, the key is to identify the candle pattern first at support or resistance. And only confirm a closed completed candle pattern.

***I use the HL30 a lot on Non Farm Payrolls

Chapter 7. Exit strategy

Here I would like to review a little more on the topic of exits and strategies.

As we mentioned earlier, looking for two profit targets for every trade is a very important component of a trading system. Almost every successful trader will exit a trade at two or three different levels.

This is applicable to any time frame. Obviously looking for two profit targets on a 30 minute chart would be a much smaller range and profit potential then what is possible on a four hour or daily chart. With the HL30 trading strategy I have meticulously calculated the distance price will typically travel after bouncing off of support or resistance on the 30 minute chart. Included Into this price calculation is where the candle pattern completes and confirms an entry.

If you choose to use this strategy on a larger time frame please do some research and calculate what a typical range is appropriate for that particular time frame after the HL30 trade system develops.

CHAPTER 8. WHY IS ONE TRADE BETTER THAN ANOTHER?

Before we move on further, I would like to share with you my thoughts on what makes one trade better than other.

I think it's important to share this with you because when you try some of these techniques you will need to determine which method to use and when to use it especially when more than one trade develops at the same time. This really comes down to being aware of the tradign environment and this wasn't easy for me to see when I first started trading.

The only way to learn how to determine market conditions is to practice and keep looking at the charts day after day.

It all comes down to the rules within your trading system.

For example if you're looking at three or four currencies trying to find a setup you might notice that at times there are certain currencies that will move opposite each other or mirror each other. This isn't the first criteria for valid trade but for the most part there are some that will behave in this manner.

So let's take the EUR/USD and the USD/CHF for example.

At the exact moment you see a potential level of support or resistance on one pair and try to translate that information to the other pair that you hope will move opposite, it could give you false signals. Often new or inexperienced traders will throw all structure and discipline out the window for the opportunity to find a trade that they cannot validate.

The key in identifying the best trading opportunity is to stay true to your trading rules.

Even if you see another currency that appears to be mirroring your currency with a valid signal, it's best to only trade the one with solid confirmation. The one that has signaled according to all of your trading rules. One such example of this scenario is explained on the charts below.

To set up this scenario, we will review how these two trades set up.

The first chart you will see in the next example is the EUR/USD Chart 1. 30 minute time frame. You'll notice that there are a total of 12 candles once the new day started which is identified by the vertical line. At the point when the 12th candle appeared it looked like the euro/USD was running into some resistance at approximately the 382 retracement from the previous downswing.

The 382 retracement level is a very popular location for traders to enter positions anticipating the continuing trend or looking for a reversal. Even though it is popular, it isn't necessarily the best location to enter. There are many things to consider and most successful traders will not recommend entering simply with price touching a certain level without confirmation.

We also know that the 382 retracement level can sometimes act as temporary support or resistance which will then soon enough give way to even further retracements. Often, price can go deeper than the 618 retracement level. This possibility creates a challenge for most. Whether they should trade from the first retracement to the 382 or wait for the 618 level? Again there are trading strategies that develop around these opportunities but require much more information to process for a valid trade signal.

This is the first example of waiting for confirmation. Both of these currency pairs in this example appeared to be setting up trading opportunities. This one (eur/usd) was just bouncing around the 382 retracement area. I don't typically get in to a trade and expect a reversal at the 382 without confirmation

EUR/USD Chart 1

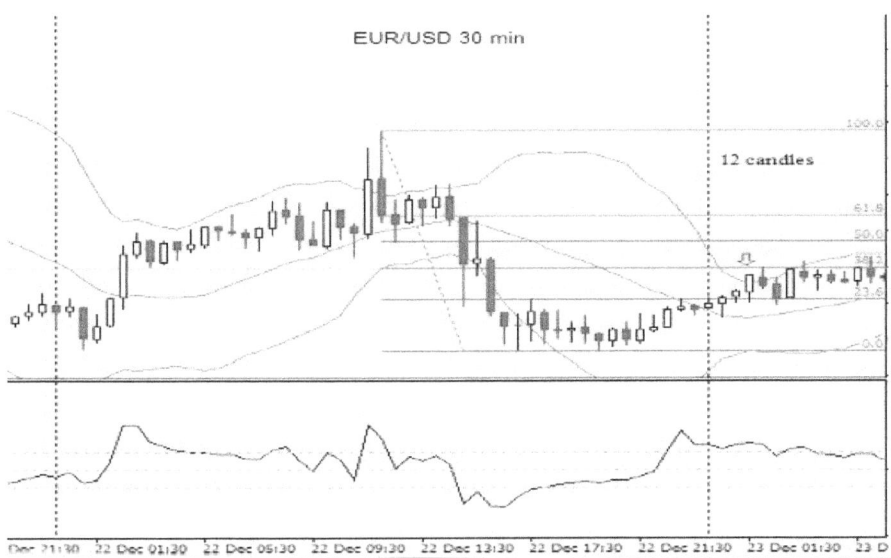

The 382 retracement level is a very popular location for traders to enter positions anticipating the continuing trend or looking for a reversal. Even though it is popular, it isn't necessarily the best location to enter. There are many things to consider and most successful traders will not recommend entering simply with price touching a certain level without confirmation.

We also know that the 382 retracement level can sometimes act as temporary support or resistance which will then soon enough give way to even further retracements. Often, price can go deeper than the 618 retracement level.

This possibility creates a challenge for most. Whether they should trade from the first retracement to the 382 or wait for the 618 level?

Again there are trading strategies that develop around these opportunities but require much more information to process for a valid trade signal.

The simplest way to identify the best trading opportunity and not get stuck in the potential of a further retracement which could stop you out using a small stop loss, is to use the one that follows all of your rules.

In this case, the USD/CHF met every trading rule when a signal was generated.

On the USD/CHF 30 minute chart you will notice 12 candles after the new day began it printed and engulfing bullish candle. This is what we like to refer to as the HL 30 trade. All forms of confirmation were met on this pair.

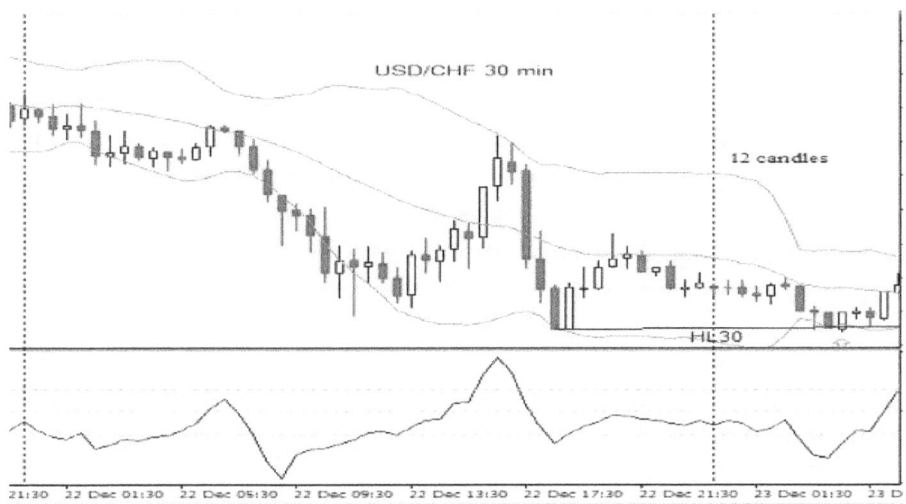

You'll notice on the second chart for the EUR/USD which was 18 candles later, price retraced higher to the 618 level. This retracement would have stopped out a trader using a stop loss of approximately 20 pips.

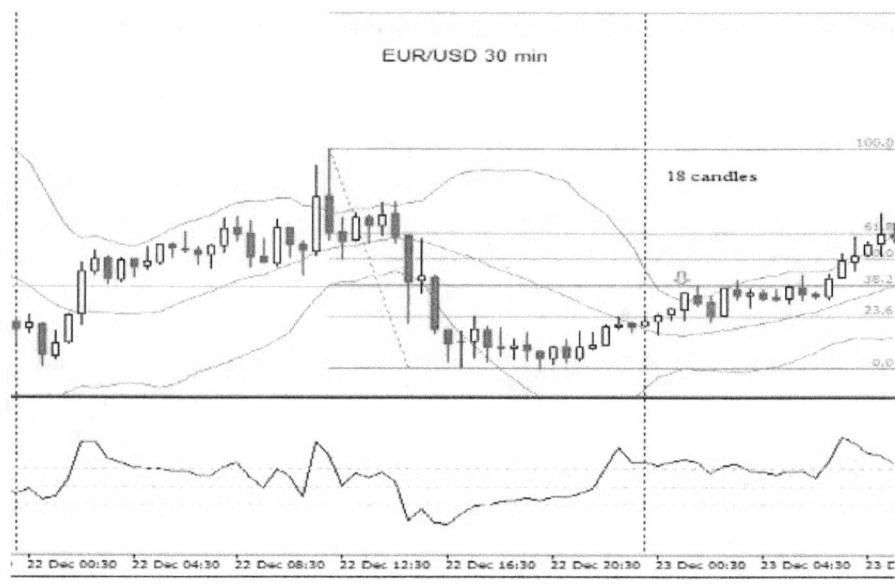

The second chart for the USD/CHF shows a retracement of the support level but nowhere near approaching the 20 pip stop loss.

USD/CHF 30 min

18 candles

HL30 ⓣ

22 Dec 00:30 22 Dec 04:30 22 Dec 08:30 22 Dec 12:30 22 Dec 16:30 22 Dec 20:30 23 Dec 00:30 23 Dec 04:30 23 D

Moving forward, the third chart for the USD/CHF shows price reaching its final target which was approximately 60 pips from the entry. This trade resulted in approximately a two for one reward to risk ratio.

There was very little to worry about during this trade.

The EUR/USD however would have required either moving the stop loss to a higher level or being stopped out completely before price ultimately moved back down towards lower levels.

Just because something looks okay doesn't mean it's the right trade. It's vitally important to confirm every aspect of the trade and make sure that it follows your rules. Each trade is either a yes or a no. In other words like an on or off switch.

CHAPTER 9. MORE ON TRADING IN THE RIGHT CONDITIONS

I have often been asked what is it that I do differently from the majority of the other traders out there that helps me remain more profitable?

I have to say that the biggest advantage I have is knowing when to STOP TRADING!

I learned the hard way meaning that I lost a lot of money before I figured when the right conditions occur for a specific trading signal. I often see one of these set ups in this ebook occur throughout the trading sessions but they don't always set up at the right place.

For example, if I see a HL30 reversal candle pattern and it develops in the middle of a consolidation range as opposed to setting up at the most significant resistance or support levels, then I would stay away from trading the HL30 pattern.

The reason is that I feel many candle patterns that develop in the middle of trading ranges are not always that reliable.

I feel that I am going to see the most reliable reaction to a specific candle pattern that develops at a major support or resistance level simply because most of the market is looking at the same thing.

I want to be trading with the market and in the same direction as everyone else. Even if that means waiting and sitting on my hands for the right trading opportunity that is more in my favor than trading price action that I don't understand and can't determine the reason for price moving in the first place.

Obviously in order to know what the optimum conditions are for a particular trade set up, it requires a great deal of testing and recording the results. Its always important to keep in mind that regardless of the technique, if you create your own trading strategy... make sure it is build on "solid market principle"

To help eliminate trading mistakes, its necessary to have a system in place that will help you determine the current state of the market... "its it trending or is it in consolidation?" This will determine the strategy to be used.

CHAPTER 10. 4 TIP CHECK LIST WHEN PLACING A HL30 TRADE

There are definitely ways to reduce the chances of a trade that fails.

Use this check list when confirming a trade

1. First identify the previous day high and low.

2. Watch for price to test the previous day high or low with in the 10 pip range. (e.g. it must not fail short of resistance by more that 10 pips or move beyond the high more than 10 pips)

3. If the price test of the previous day high or low confirms then wait for the closed completed candle pattern on the 30 minute chart.

4. Once the closed completed candle pattern is confirmed then the CCI indicator must be confirmed before placing the trade. (e.g. the CCI measurement should be lower on the closed candle pattern than the previous day high candle on a short trade and higher on a long trade)

HL30 Trading System Trade Check Sheet

Okay, so you think you found a trade?!

Before you place the trade please make sure of the following:

- Did you set a vertical line on your 30 minute chart at the 5 pm eastern time (new york time) start of the new day?

- Make sure you are using the 30 minute chart

- Make sure you identify the weeks high and low

Trade criteria:

- Has price tested the previous day high or low within the 10 pip range?
  If so, move to next step, if not consider skipping the trade and looking for the next one

- Has a closed completed candle pattern appeared? (bullish or bearish engulfing candle pattern, evening or morning star pattern)
  If so, move to next step, if not consider skipping the trade and looking for the next one

- Do you have CCI confirmation? (CCI must be set at 14) e.g. lower CCI measurement on a bearish set up, higher CCI measurement on a bullish set up

Entry is on the close of the completed candle pattern is all criteria is confirmed:

- EUR/USD uses a 20 pip target with a 20 pip stop loss

- GBP/USD uses a 20 pip target with a 20 pip stop loss

- EUR/JPY and GBP/JPY use a 40 pip target with a 40 pip stop loss

5 Mistakes to avoid when placing a trade

There are definitely ways to reduce the chances of a trade that fails and here we will take a look at 5 of the most common...

1. Failure to determine trend direction by using the larger times frames such as the 4 hour, daily and weekly charts.

2. Failure to determine an exact entry point before placing the trade. It usually isn't recommended to simply jump in a trade just because price may be rallying at the time. Often, this type of behavior leads to uncertainty and without a clear entry point, finding a place to take profits may be just as unclear.

3. Failure to determine potential profit target before placing the trade. It is important that you have a clear profit target before you get into a trade.

4. Failure to be aware of any economic announcement that can have an impact on your trade.

5. Failure to identify significant support and resistance levels that can only be seen by using the larger time frames. Often, traders hold on to a profitable trade too long expecting more and this can ultimately lead to a failed trade.

I hope you enjoyed this report.   -Joseph

ABOUT THE AUTHOR

AUTHOR NAME is Joseph Fibonacci

Find out more about me on my author page on Amazon

http://www.amazon.com/-/e/B01DOQZPG0

or visit my website   www.howtomakemoneytradingforex.com

If you would like to get a FREE video tutorial trading course for the HL30 technique please visit the link below.

You can also download a full pfd manual of this exact ebook.

Click here to get your free trading course for the HL30

http://the4xcoach.com/amzminicourse/

OTHER BOOKS BY JOSEPH FIBONACCI

My current book listing on Amazon (click on the title)

- How to make 1000 pips per month and keep it

- How to trade the HL30 Technique -Forex Day Trading

Coming Soon:

- The Only Trade That Matters: How to overcome the three biggest problems that stop every trader from success. Step by step strategy to successfully trading every day and never have another losing month again!

CAN I ASK A FAVOR?

If you enjoyed this book, found it useful or otherwise then I'd really appreciate it if you would post a short review on Amazon. I do read all the reviews personally so that I can continually write what people are wanting.

If you'd like to leave a review then please visit the link below:

http://amzn.com/B01DOQR8XS

Thanks for your support!

www.ingramcontent.com/pod-product-compliance
Lightning Source LLC
Chambersburg PA
CBHW070415190526
45169CB00003B/1263